Discover and Share

Human Body

Deborah Chancellor

FRANKLIN WATTS
LONDON•SYDNEY

About this book

The **Discover and Share** series enables young readers to read about familiar topics independently. The books are designed to build on children's existing knowledge while providing new information and vocabulary. By sharing this book, either with an adult or another child, young children can learn how to access information, build word recognition skills and develop reading confidence in an enjoyable way.

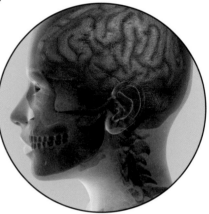

Reading tips

👤 Begin by finding out what children already know about the topic. Encourage them to talk about it and take the opportunity to introduce vocabulary specific to the topic.

👤 Each image is explained through two levels of text. Confident readers will be able to read the higher level text independently, while emerging readers can try reading the simpler sentences.

👤 Check for understanding of any unfamiliar words and concepts. Inexperienced readers might need you to read some or all of the text to them. Encourage children to retell the information in their own words.

👤 After you have explored the book together, try the quiz on page 22 to see what children can remember and to encourage further discussion.

Contents

Words in **bold** are in the glossary on page 23.

Amazing body

Your body is amazing! Each part of it has a job to do and works with other parts to keep you alive and well.

Your body is made up of about 65 billion tiny **cells**. Every single one is a building block for a particular part of your body, such as your brain or heart.

Your body is amazing! It is made
up of billions of tiny cells like these. 5

Super skeleton

You have lots of bones in your skeleton. If you break a bone, it will mend itself.

Your skeleton holds up your body and protects your **organs**. You have over 200 bones in your skeleton. The places where they join together are called joints.

If you break
a bone, you can
see the damage
on an X-ray.
A broken bone
should be bandaged
and kept still. It will
mend itself in time.

On the move

You have more
than 600 **muscles**
in your body.
They help you
to move and
keep your body
working.

Your muscles keep your body moving. They make your heart beat and help your lungs breathe in and out.

You have more than 600 muscles. Over 40 of them are in your face. Humans can pull more faces than any other kind of animal!

Pumping power

Your heart is a bag of muscle about as big as your fist. It pumps blood around your body.

Your blood carries **oxygen** and **nutrients** to cells all over your body to give you energy to move. It also takes waste away from these cells.

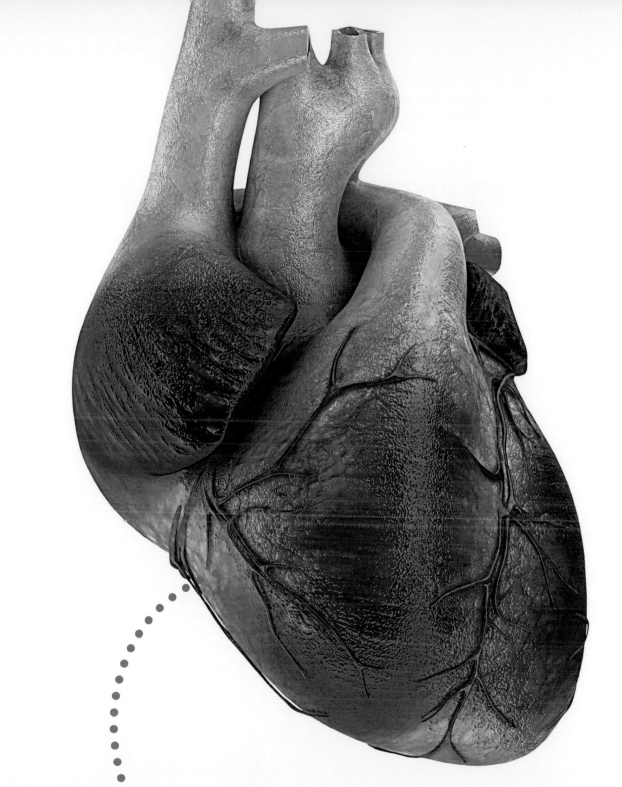

**Your heart is about as big as your fist.
It pumps blood around your body.**

Hard work

Your organs all have important jobs to do.
Your skin is your biggest organ.
It protects you from **germs**.

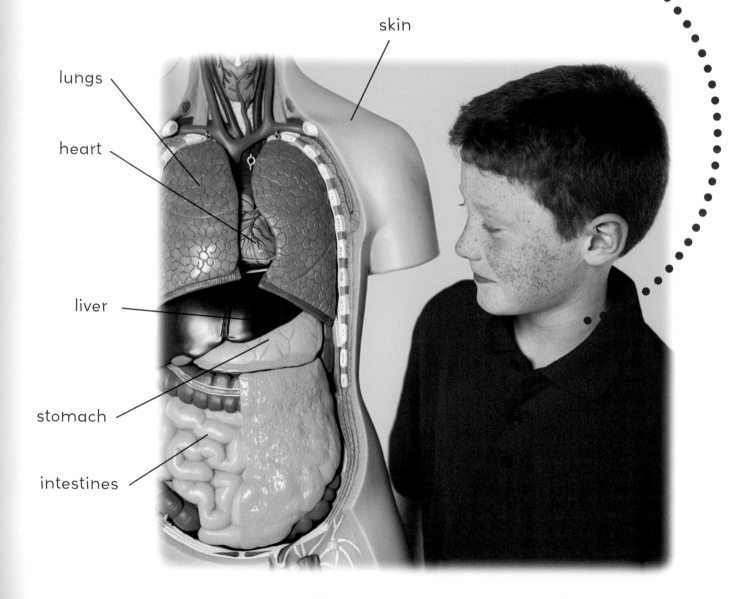

skin

lungs

heart

liver

stomach

intestines

Your organs never stop working, even when you are asleep. Your heart still pumps blood, your lungs breathe air, your intestines **digest** food and your liver and kidneys sort waste.

Your organs all have jobs to do. They work even when you are asleep.

Eat for energy

Your body breaks down the food you eat.

This gives you energy and keeps you well.

14

When you eat food, your body breaks it down so it can be carried round in your blood. This gives you energy and nutrients.

Your teeth, **saliva**, stomach and intestines all help to break down your food. This is called digestion. It begins when you chew food and ends when you go to the toilet.

Control centre

Your brain is in charge of your body! It sends out messages telling your body what to do.

Tiny threads called nerves carry the messages to every single part of your body. Messages come back through the nerves, telling your brain what is happening to your body.

**Your brain controls
what you do. It sends messages
around your body.**

Making sense

Your five senses tell you about the world. You see with your eyes, hear with your ears, touch with your skin, smell with your nose and taste with your tongue and nose.

Your senses send your brain messages, so you can **react** to what is happening around you.

You have five senses. They help you to see, hear, taste, smell and touch.

Keeping well

Some kinds of food help your body grow and mend. Other kinds give you energy, or help you digest your dinner. Eat different kinds of food to stay healthy. Drink plenty of water, too.

20

Take some exercise every day
to keep well. Your body also needs
to rest, so get lots of sleep at night.

Eat different kinds of food to keep your body healthy. Take exercise every day and get lots of sleep!

Quiz

1. How many bones are in your skeleton?

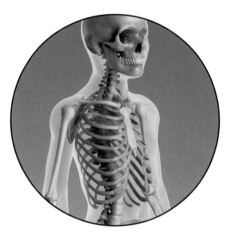

2. What does your heart do?

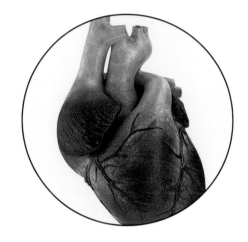

3. What are your muscles for?

4. What are your five senses?

Glossary

cell the smallest living part of your body

digest to break down food in your body

germs tiny living things that can make you ill

muscle a part of your body that makes you move

nutrient goodness in food that helps your
body to work and grow

organ a part of your body with an important
job to do, such as your heart

oxygen a gas in the air you must breathe in to stay alive

react to behave in a particular way because
something is happening

saliva the spit in your mouth

skeleton the structure of bones inside your body

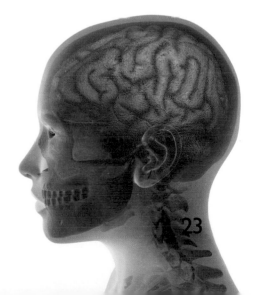

Answers to the quiz:
1. You have over 200 bones
in your skeleton.
2. It pumps blood around your body.
3. They keep your body moving and
your organs working
4. Sight, hearing, touch, taste, smell.

23

Index

First published in 2015 by
Franklin Watts
338 Euston Road
London
NW1 3BH

Franklin Watts Australia
Level 17/207 Kent Street
Sydney
NSW 2000

Copyright © Franklin Watts 2015

HB ISBN 978 1 4451 3795 7
Library ebook ISBN 978 1 4451 3796 4

Dewey number: 611

A CIP catalogue record for this book is
available from the British Library.

Series Editor: Julia Bird
Series Advisor: Karina Law
Series Design: Basement68

Picture credits: Richard Bailey/SPL/Alamy: 3t, 12. bikeriderlondon/Shutterstock:
3c, 13. Scott Camazine/Alamy: 2, 16. Jacek Chabraszewski/Shutterstock: front
cover. Konstantin Christian/Shutterstock: 19, 22br. CulturaRM/Alamy: 5. Ikurugan/
Shutterstock: 8, 22bl. infocus/Shutterstock: 14. Sebastian Kaulitzki/Dreamstime: 11,
22tr. Jo Millington/Shutterstock: 9. Monkey Business Images/Shutterstock: 1, 20,
21. Sergey Novikov/Shutterstock: 4. Oliveromg/Shutterstock: 10. Percival ITSB24/
Alamy: 18. racorn/Shutterstock: 3b, 17. Science Picture Co/Alamy: 6, 22tl. Don
Smith/Alamy: 15. Terry Vine/Blend Images/Alamy: 7.

Printed in China

Franklin Watts is a division of
Hachette Children's Books,
an Hachette UK company.
www.hachette.co.uk